# DAVE HUNT
# UNDERSTANDING THE NEW AGE MOVEMENT

**HARVEST HOUSE PUBLISHERS**
Eugene, Oregon 97402

## UNDERSTANDING THE NEW AGE MOVEMENT

Taken from **PEACE, PROSPERITY, AND THE COMING HOLOCAUST**
Copyright © 1983 by Dave Hunt
Published by Harvest House Publishers
Eugene, Oregon 97402

ISBN 0-89081-682-4

# Contents

# 1

# *A New World Order*

A new kind of revolution is quietly taking over planet Earth. Unlike the Russian Revolution and other violent uprisings that installed new governments in the past, this revolution will conquer without guns. As New Age Movement leaders would say: "The new politics is involved more with . . . getting in touch with our 'Higher Self,' more with mysticism than violence. . . ." It is a "consciousness revolution."

This new world order is actually a religion, though it often wears a political mask. Its millions of sincere participants have adopted an ecumenical faith that will form the basis of the coming world religion: belief in the oneness of all life and in themselves as part of the Universal Self or Consciousness. They fervently believe that an awakening of brotherhood and love will usher in a new age of peace, prosperity, and incredible progress. As evidence of this, they point to a new and world phenomenon that was first ignited by the drug culture and then expanded through the

5

spread of Eastern meditation techniques in the West: the emergence of a new "planetary consciousness" in human beings. As Mark Satin says in *New Age Politics*:

> Planetary consciousness recognizes our oneness . . . with all life everywhere and with the planet . . . the interdependence of all humanity. . . .
> Planetary consciousness sees each of us as "cells in the body of humanity," as Planetary Citizens.
> . . . we are beginning to see the emergence of a new *collective* consciousness.[1]

## The Aquarian Network

Marilyn Ferguson has called this movement *The Aquarian Conspiracy*. Many others agree with her in identifying the new age as the Age of Aquarius. New age thinking involves a new "openness" to one another, to ourselves, to nature, to a universal "Force" pervading the whole cosmos—which allegedly produces an awakening of unimagined powers of the mind. Playing an important role in the new age, astrology is based upon a belief in this interconnectedness, which determines personality and destiny depending upon the date and location of one's birth in relation to certain heavenly bodies. Like Hinduism, upon which it is based, the Aquarian Conspiracy claims to embrace all beliefs, all religions, on the premise that all is one. Dealing

with the question "Is nuclear war in our future?"
New Age astrologer Virginia Kay Miller declared:

> . . . the world is in the midst of a massive upheaval.
>
> . . . many people believe that human-mankind is on the verge of an evolutionary break-through and we are standing on the threshold of a New Age.
>
> Called the "Aquarian Age," it will bring about a new world order in which individuals will realize their true spiritual being and their interconnectedness with all life.
>
> To survive . . . as a planet, we must develop the Aquarian consciousness, which recognizes that we are all linked together as members of the human race and as inhabitants of planet Earth.
>
> We must network. . . .[2]

"Network" is a New Age code word that refers not to radio or television but to the thousands of groups around the world that are all working toward the realization of this "interconnectedness" of all life through the establishment of a world government. Many of these networks expect the United Nations one day to function as the "central nervous system" in the new world order. This new planetary consciousness is shared by many leaders, who often express their belief in almost-mystical terms. Robert Muller, long-time Assistant Secretary-General of the United Nations and an avid networker, has said: "This old planet and the human species on it are

[like] . . . a big brain whose neurons are multiplying incessantly, encompassing everything from the individual to the planet, to humanity and the universe . . . The world brain is already so complicated . . . new interconnections are being created so rapidly . . . [it] is a new biological phenomenon, one of the most momentous ones in the earth's history. . . .[3] As the authors of *Networking: The First Report and Directory* declared:

> We went looking for networks, and we found . . . a significant American subculture with values oriented to human transformation and global peace.[4]

Networks are composed of hundreds and sometimes thousands of groups. There are "New Age caucuses . . . trying to work for New Age-oriented change-and-transformation from within our already established social, cultural, economic and professional organizations and institutions . . . [such as] the Social Change Network of the Association for Humanistic Psychology. . . .[5] There are "New Age business and professional organizations . . . [such as] the Transpersonal Association for World Education. New Age discussion groups are springing up across the country: the Political Science Committee of the Institute for the New Age and New Age Feminism . . . New Age education groups . . . the Hunger Project, Planetary Citizens, Movement for a New Society" and a host of others.[6] The list is almost endless.

## Planetary Conspirators

Marilyn Ferguson insists that the New Age Movement "is not a new political, religious, or philosophical system. It is a new mind—the ascendance of a startling world view that gathers into its framework break-through science and insights from earliest recorded thought."[7] "Insights from earliest recorded thought" is a euphemistic way of referring to ancient occultism. The "new mind" that Ms. Ferguson speaks of comes about through acceptance of basic Hindu philosophy, which is the cement that holds together the otherwise seemingly disparate views of this new world religion. And it *is* political, for the common goal is a new world order, a world government.

The Association for Global Education, Cooperation, and Accreditation declares: "Only by the birth of global consciousness within each individual can we truly achieve trans-nationalization."[8] As the Servers' Network has declared, we are indeed witnessing the "emergence of a new universal person and civilization."[9] The normal loyalty to the nation of one's birth is being overturned in favor of "planetary citizenship." That this is being advocated by sincere persons under the stress of the dire emergencies we face and in order to save our species from extinction is not doubted. Much of the energy, time, and attention expended by those in the New Age Movement is directed inward, getting "in touch with themselves" and with their "feelings" in order to find out who they really are. The new global consciousness is based upon the experience of "unity consciousness" that comes through drugs or TM and other forms of Yoga and Eastern meditation, and leads to the Hindu belief that atman (individual soul) is identical with Brahman (universal soul). This is a denial of the Judeo-Christian God of the Bible in exchange for the belief that we are all "God." This ancient Hindu belief is being accepted today as non-religious modern science. By a handful of naive fanatics? No, by millions of well-educated sophisticates.

The range and scope and influence of the New Age Movement is worldwide and truly awesome. No one lays it out as well as Marilyn Ferguson:

> The Aquarian Conspirators range across all levels of income and education . . . schoolteachers and office workers, famous scientists, government officials and lawmakers, artists and millionaires, taxi drivers and celebrities, leaders in medicine, education, law, psychology. . . .
>
> They have coalesced into small groups in every town and institution. They [are effecting a] . . . social transformation that is increasingly visible if you know where to look. . . .
>
> There are tens of thousands of entry points to this conspiracy.[10]

## What New Age Movement?

Of course, not everyone takes the New Age

Movement seriously. Some deny that it even exists. "What New Age Movement?" is a common remark. While almost everyone will have noticed the words "New Age" appearing with increasing frequency, not many people recognized the coherent pattern involved, and fewer still understand what the words really mean, much less their great importance in shaping the future of humanity and this planet. In fact, many New Agers are scarcely aware of the full implications of their involvement in the movement. And because the movement is more an organism than an organization, many people would vehemently deny that they are involved at all.

Most people outside the movement who recognize its existence sincerely believe that it is limited to a few visionaries whose impact upon society will be very minimal at most. Nothing could be further from the truth! Suggesting that the New Age Movement may in fact exist "largely in Marilyn Ferguson's head," Stanford University history professor Paul Robinson criticizes her *Aquarian Conspiracy* as "an exercise in mindlessness" that obliterates "most of what our civilization has achieved" in its "thoughtless pages."[11] Yet the Stanford University faculty itself includes a number of New Age leaders such as professors Willis Harman, William Tiller and Michael Ray.

Robinson's harsh judgment is a typical materialist denunciation that recognizes only the rational aspects of the brain and rejects as deception or delusion the apparent paranormal powers of the mind. New Agers, however, believe they can develop *transpersonal* or so-called *transcendent* powers of the mind—those seemingly supernatural or Godlike powers that the Yogis, shamans, witch doctors, and voodoo priests have always manifested. While science has traditionally viewed psychic phenomena with suspicion and skepticism, recently ESP, psychokinesis, telepathy, clairvoyance, and other such powers have been scientifically demonstrated. Therefore, the New Age belief in these "powers of the mind" simply cannot be dismissed as "mindlessness" in the cavalier manner with which Robinson attempts to write them off. Their position must be taken seriously, not ridiculed; and the evidence must be examined carefully. This we intend to do.

First of all, however, we need to understand that the New Age Movement is based upon beliefs that have always been regarded instinctively by the human race as witchcraft and demonism. We agree with Robinson that Ferguson and other New Agers have been too easily convinced that the "mind powers" they seek are desirable. In fact, these may not be "mind powers" at all—at least not the capabilities of *human* minds!

Whether real or imagined, and whatever the explanation, through "altered states of consciousness" paranormal "mind powers" have been experienced by millions of people in the West under the stimulation of drugs, Yoga, hypnosis, Eastern meditation, etc. These experiences of alleged "mind powers" seem so real that all of the rational arguments or ridicule of a Paul Robinson have little effect on New Agers.

As a result, the Hindu monistic view of reality has become the predominant world view in the West today. It exerts a strong influence in science, medicine, psychology, sociology, education, politics, business—and especially in feminism, which is in the forefront of the New Age Movement.

## The Women's Movement

In universities across America, a new group of courses called "women's studies" has come into existence within the past decade. There are "women's studies departments" in our colleges and "centers for feminist therapy" in our cities and suburbs. The national attention that was given to the Equal Rights Amendment campaign failed to mention that the major force behind it was spiritual, not political, and is still gaining momentum. The Women's Movement, as one of the most important parts of the New Age Movement, is at the heart of the consciousness revolution that is sweeping the Western world. As Berkeley physicist Fritjof Capra has said:

> Like the Cartesian paradigm, patriarchy is now on the decline. And I believe that the rise of Feminist awareness is one of the most important aspects of the emerging new vision of reality.[12]

Many of those involved in the Feminist Movement may sincerely believe it is a political crusade to gain equality with men. In fact it is more than that: it is also a spiritual movement based upon a reawakening of "goddess consciousness." One major spiritual force behind some aspects of the feminist movement is witchcraft, which is based upon the power of female sexuality derived from a mystical relation with "Mother Nature" and "Mother Earth."

Take, for example a women's conference held in Southern California entitled "Women: The Leading Edge of the New Age." Declared Linda Barone, the feminist therapist who organized the conference: "The New Age will allow us to experience a sense of wholeness, a sense of connectedness with nature" (i.e., Mother Nature).[13] Any witch would immediately recognize the significance of that statement. However, for those who don't know that "nature religion" is witchcraft, the movement often spells it out more clearly. One brochure from the Universal Goddess Center, Inc., encourages women "to express their 'new' spirituality—which is the oldest on earth."

As any witch will proudly inform you, the oldest spirituality on earth is Wicca or witchcraft. Who would suspect that *new* spirituality means *oldest spirituality*, or that *higher* states of consciousness are really *lower* states, sinking ever deeper within the "Self"? The New Age Movement employs words and phrases that seem to mean one thing but actually mean something entirely different to insiders. "God" in the New Age is the pantheistic god of ancient paganism, the All of Hinduism, and *not* the transcendent God of the Judeo-Christian Bible. Thus "transcendental meditation," which is pure Hinduism posing as science, is a deceptive label that really means the opposite: *subscendence* ever deeper into oneself. The "new" psychic powers being verified in some of our top laboratories today, from Harvard and Princeton to Stanford and UCLA, are really the *old* occult powers that Yogis, shamans, witch doctors and voodoo priests have always exhibited. "New Age" is a euphemism for "old occultism." And this is nowhere seen more clearly than in the "new spirituality" advocated by many leaders in the Women's Movement.

## Goddess of the New Age

One popular seminar at a large, typical "Women's Spirituality & Healing Conference" was titled "Introduction to Goddess Consciousness and the Craft." One would have to be very naive not to know that "the Craft" is *witchcraft*. Included in that workshop were discussions of "goddess consciousness . . . nymph, maiden, crone; the Sacred Wheel; politics of women's celebrations; how do spells and rituals work?" Other seminars included "Pathways to Your Inner Light" ("meet your own spiritual guides, and discover the light within . . . harmonize your mental, physical, emotional and spiritual levels of beingness through hypnosis and meditation"); "Medicine Wheel Magic"; "How to Enjoy the Present by Experiencing Past and Future Lives"; "Female Erotic Power and Orgasmic Responses"; and "In The Beginning Was the Goddess." The brochure described this last seminar as follows:

In this workshop, women will discover their own lost heritage by exploring ancient concepts of deity as "goddess." Although the great Mother Goddess was worshipped everywhere in the world for more than 10,000 years *before* the concept of male gods emerged in human consciousness, She is little known [today].

More than 200 slides of images of various aspects of the universal Goddess will be shown, their psychological and spiritual ramifications for our lives and for our time will be discussed, and the positive benefits of incorporating into our value structure a feminine image of the divine will be explored.

Under the heading "GODDESSES OF COMING NEW AGE PROBE THE MEANING OF IT ALL," *Los Angeles Times* staff writer Elizabeth Mehren reported on a March 1982 gathering of leaders in the Women's Movement.[14] Among those present was Charlene Spretnak, who declared: "I believe that women are the teachers in society's transformation into the New Age." Past-lives therapist Jean Whitaker, transpersonal psychologist Jackie Holley, and former cloistered nun Patricia James, now the guru and director of the Awareness Ashram in Echo Park, Los Angeles, were there explaining the importance of the Women's Movement in the New Age.

Malka Golden-Wolfe, founder of the Universal Goddess Center in Malibu, California, and former aide to Los Angeles Mayor Tom Bradley, declared in no uncertain terms that "the healing of the planet depends upon women." She explained that through going "deeper into myself" she discovered the "guru and the teacher and the mother within all of us."[15] The goals of the movement are pretty well summed up in a 590-page book of feminist writings edited by Charlene Spretnak, *The Politics of Women's Spirituality*, which a reviewer described in part as follows:

> The particular brand of spirituality championed in the book as the hope of the world is the ancient goddess worship that characterized a supposedly bygone Golden Age of matriarchal rule.
>
> Goddess worship, paganism, Wicca, and witchcraft are all names for a form of natural religion that is centered around the mystery, sexuality, and psychic abilities of the female.
>
> The book is a clarion call to women to regain their natural power and to overthrow the global rule of men. The authors' starting point for the reestablishment of female dominance is in bringing an end to Judeo-Christian religion.[16]

The New Age Movement professes a broadminded openness to all religions, but its basic underlying philosophy represents a carefully calculated undermining of Judeo-Christian beliefs, a rejection of the Judeo-Christian God, and the declaration that Self is God.

# 2

# *Health, Self, and Science*

As we have already seen, the New Age employs euphemisms in order to disguise the religion behind it. Words like witchcraft, spiritism, animism, and voodoo still have "bad vibes" and connotations of ignorance and superstition. "Traditional" sounds so much better: it has an aura of broad-minded acceptance of "native" cultures without judging them; and getting back to one's roots is currently in vogue. For those who are still struggling to shake off Judeo-Christian morality learned in childhood, the euphemism "traditional" covers a multitude of sins.

As a means of easing the burden on modern health-care systems, the World Health Organization (WHO) of the United Nations has given offical approval to "traditional healers" around the world. In Bulawayo, Zimbabwe, for example, Dr. Bingara Tshuma, "a consultant traditional healer who shares a medical center with two conventional, Western-trained doctors, straightens his animal skin headdress, removes his shoes, inhales snuff through both nostrils and wills himself into a hypnotic trance."[1] He then calls upon his spirit guide to advise him. "People who come here have a choice between the *nganga* [traditional healer] or the doctors," says Babra Sibanda, a registered nurse who owns the Zimbabwe Medical and Traditional Practitioners' Center. "But the *nganga* is the busiest of our consultants. Even whites choose to go to him."[2] There are about 8000 licensed "traditional healers" in Zimbabwe alone, who "pass on their secrets —and their spirits—from father to son or mother to daughter, and claim to be able to cure most illnesses."[3] To New Agers, "spirits" is a "native" word for the "mind powers" that lie within us all.

### Euphemistic Exorcism

It is not merely the word "traditional" that exorcises witchcraft and spiritism of its old demonic connotations. Witchcraft and shamanistic powers, which have always been instinctively recognized as *demonic*, are today called psychic and are accepted even by science. Under the new labels, leading scientists (who formerly rejected witchcraft and spiritism as pagan superstition) are now "discovering" real power in "traditional" techniques.

Zimbabwe's deputy health minister, Dr. Simon Mazorodze, has said, "These traditional healers have a lot to teach us, especially in the field of mental health."[4] A recent "experiment at the

All-India Institute of Mental Health in Bangalore found that Western-trained psychiatrists and native [traditional] faith healers had a comparable recovery rate. The most notable difference was that the so-called 'witchdoctors' released their patients sooner!"[5] This should not have been surprising. Long before this test was conducted, world-renowned research psychiatrist E. Fuller Torrey in his book *Mind Games* declared: "The methods of Western psychiatrists, with few exceptions, are on the same scientific plane as the methods of witchdoctors."

## Selfism and Occultism

If "all is One," as New Age consciousness tells us, then evil is good, God and Satan are One, and everything there is can be found within the Self. Marilyn Ferguson writes, "The search for self becomes a search for health, for wholeness. . . ."[6] Americans spend 100 billion dollars annually on health care, which is about one month's salary for every worker in America! No other nation even comes close to this. Psychology and the New Age Movement have obsessed us with self. Within three pages, Ferguson mentions "a new understanding of self," "multiple dimensions of self," the "merger with a Self yet more universal," "self-knowledge," "redefining the self," the "self released," an "unapologetic self," an "even larger Self," the "collective Self," and a "transcendent, universal Self."[7] Martin L. Gross says:

We live in a civilization in which, as never before, man is preoccupied with *Self.* . . .

. . . as the Protestant ethic has weakened in Western society, the confused citizen has turned to the only alternative he knows: the psychological expert who claims there is a *new scientific standard of behavior* to replace fading traditions. . . .

Mouthing the holy name of science, the psychological expert claims to know all.

This new truth is fed to us continuously from birth to the grave. . . . The schoolhouse has become a vibrant psychological center. . . . The need for psychological expertise follows us doggedly through life.[8]

Western psychologists and psychiatrists are the gurus of the 1980's, leading us into New Age mysticism. Under their direction, we have believed the serpent's lie and have mistaken ourselves for God. Carl Jung wrote, "I have called this centre the *self*. It might equally well be called the 'God within us' "[9] Abraham Maslow's "Self-actualization" is Hinduism's "Self-realization" thinly veiled in the jargon of humanistic psychology. Maslow said, "Therefore, if the individual can touch these depths within himself . . . he discovers not only himself, but also the whole human spirit. The nonacademic psychologists [witch doctors] of the East have always known this; we in the West must learn it too."[10]

## New Age Thinking for Businessmen

Within the past two decades, the "down-with-the-establishment" and "up-with-me" attitude in the West has taken a mystical leap to the East. Selfism has now become the new panacea of medicine, psychiatry, sociology, politics, once-materialistic science, and even of business. When the pragmatic, profit-oriented businessman has embraced selfism as the most up-to-date, scientific method of achieving his goals, then we are very far down the road indeed. Training in New Age thinking has taken the Bell Telephone System (AT&T) by storm, beginning with top executives and working its way down through all levels and finally to families and retirees. Ferguson exults:

> One Aquarian Conspirator who works with top management people around the country refers to the new "businessmen-philosophers" who talk to each other until three in the morning about their own changing values and their discoveries of human potential. . . .
>
> Big business . . . is becoming aware of the networks of the Aquarian Conspiracy. . . .
>
> . . . one such underground network [is described] . . . whose main orientation is radical science and transpersonal psychology and whose photo copying is furnished by the vice-chairman of American Telephone and Telegraph.[11]

Like millions of people in every other area of society, businessmen are finding the secret to greater happiness and success, at least temporarily, through scores of different self-help and success seminars. Typical would be Lifespring, which is very similar to The Forum, formerly est (Erhard Seminars Training). Most of these courses are a blend of humanistic psychology and Eastern mysticism, making them part of the New Age Movement. Lifespring's philosophy is basically the same as that of Leo Buscaglia or W. Brugh Joy: "At the essence, or core, of each of us is a perfect, loving, and caring being . . . each of us already has everything necessary to achieve and be all we want in our lives . . . we literally create our experience of life based upon our beliefs about ourselves and how we expect the universe to react to us."[12]

The revival of occultism that began in drugs and moved on into Eastern mysticism has become pervasive throughout our society. Experiences that would have been frightening to almost anyone ten years ago are taken for granted today. One top nuclear physicist confessed at a cocktail party that he receives some of his most brilliant ideas out in space, where he sometimes finds himself "out-of-body" and in the company of other scientists being taught advanced concepts by spirit beings. Of course, in the New Age, very few really believe in spirit beings. Although they may be called that for convenience, they are considered to be a mysterious manifestation of one's own infinite Self.

## New Age Technology

Western technology has invented, designed, manufactured, and marketed commercial devices for automatically producing the so-called "higher" states of consciousness that open the door to occult experiences and psychic powers. What used to take a powerful dose of LSD or months of Yoga meditation and vegetarianism can now be accomplished in a few minutes through new devices that are multiplying at an alarming rate. Biofeedback was one of the first such mechanisms. The Menninger Clinic of Topeka, Kansas, has a promotional film titled "Biofeedback, the Yoga of the West." In other words, biofeedback puts you into the same state of consciousness and develops the same control over involuntary bodily functions—and the same occult experiences and psychic powers—that have always been the stock in trade of great Yogis. Reflecting their Hindu-Buddhist occult world view, Elmer and Alyce Green, of the Menninger Clinic, leading authorities on biofeedback, write:

> In working with patients we do not often point out that the "detachment" to which we refer is a basic feature of yogic training. . . . There are other similarities between biofeedback training and yoga.

> I guided myself through the development of these ideas by the intentional use of hypnogogic imagery. Whenever I was "stuck" I made my mind a blank and asked the unconscious to get the information I needed from wherever it was, from . . . the collective mind, or from the "future". . . .[13]

Another ingenious product to take advantage of the new consciousness boom is the isolation/ flotation tank. In order to find relief from the stress in our modern world, participants "float in an isolated, weightless and soundproof environment."[14] One Beverly Hills firm called Samadhi, Inc., is producing about 600 of these tanks per month, which sell for about 3500 dollars each. Inside the tank one is entirely isolated from sight and sound, floating alone in an Epsom salt solution. Heartbeat and breathing cause the body to move erratically, which, together with the sense of weightlessness, creates an altered state of consciousness that can produce out-of-body experiences and develop psychic powers. "Psychologist Eleanor Portner, of Pacific Palisades, uses the tank for patient therapy and says, 'Taking away the external stimuli enables someone to move toward the core, their self.' "[15] Another psychologist, however, cautions that "it can be dangerous for some people to come in touch with themselves."[16] One wonders why that should be, if it is really only oneself one is coming in contact with. Could it be something else?

## Science Over the Cliff

Swami Rama, star performer at the Menninger Clinic and founder of the Himalayan Institute of Yoga Science, has been sponsoring an annual "International Congress of Yoga, Meditation and Holistic Health" in Chicago since 1976. In 1978, the inaugural speaker was New Age leader Buckminster Fuller, world-renowned innovator and architect and a leading spokesman for the cosmic gospel. The speakers presented to the large audience a blend of Hinduism and Western science suitable for a new world religion. President Carter sent a message wishing the participants of the congress well. In part it read:

> The constructive melding of Eastern and Western philosophies and the practice [of this blend] in the medical and health field can be of considerable importance to society and to the well-being of all mankind.

In fact, the invasion of the West by Hindu-Buddhist philosophies is destroying lives here just as it has in the East. Participants in the 1977 Congress explained the "ancient wisdom" of Eastern mysticism and what it would do in developing our full potential. Kabbalist Rabbi J. Gelberman said, "God can't do anything without me." "Our nature is identical with that of God," added Yogiraj Roy E. Davis. Chitrabhanu declared, "The belief that you are a sinner hinders your growth"; and Jagdish Dave affirmed, "My consciousness is God." The following words from Jonathan Stone were prophetic:

> I feel that there is coming a world order in which science will merge with monistic philosophy and all the world will be swept up in a new consciousness.
>
> The one distinguishing feature in that world order will be the credo: "All is one."[17]

That is exactly where science is heading at breakneck speed. Fritjof Capra wrote *The Tao of*

*Physics* and *The Turning Point* to show "how the revolution in modern physics foreshadows an imminent revolution in all the sciences and a transformation of our world view and values."[18]

Because of a mystical experience during the Apollo 14 moon trip, Edgar Mitchell abandoned the exploration of outer space to join the exploration of inner space, the pursuit of the Self or the "God" within. This is the new frontier of science. Increasing numbers of scientists today reason that we can explore the universe by going deep within ourselves, journeying through "inner space" to contact this Universal Self. This is the old occultism, which is fast becoming new science.

# 3

# New Age Education

New Age educators use the term "values clarification" as a euphemism in our public schools to hide their deliberate rebellion against moral absolutes. "Clarification" of values is designed to do away with Judeo-Christian morals by denying that there is any absolute standard available for measuring moral values. Obviously, if there is no objective measurement, then the very word "values" becomes meaningless. In rejection of the Judeo-Christian moral absolutes taught in the Bible (that derive from the personal Creator-God), "values clarification" encourages the student to look within himself for "inner guidance." The only thing that matters is how the student "feels" about a situation. Above all, he must be "true to himself" and not succumb to the pressure of the opinions of others, the taboos of society, or religious standards. What is actually happening, however, is that the unsuspecting student is being conditioned to accept New Age values! And in most cases the parents are just as unsuspecting of what is really happening to their children in the process of public school education.

In his fascinating book *The Abolition of Man*, C. S. Lewis referred to an elementary school textbook of his day which was supposed to teach English to school children. However, it was in reality a calculated attempt to undermine a belief in any moral values outside the individual's own preferences and feelings. It was also designed to condition the unsuspecting students to accept the "values" presented in the textbook. What Lewis had to say in his day is apropos to hundreds of dangerous New Age textbooks today:

> The very power of [the authors] depends on the fact that they are dealing with a boy; a boy who thinks he is "doing" his "English prep" and has no notion that ethics, theology, and politics are all at stake.
>
> It is not a theory they put into his mind, but an assumption, which ten years hence, its origin forgotten and its presence unconscious, will condition him.[1]

Much like the book that C. S. Lewis describes above, but far more persuasive and dangerous, Beverly Galyean's *Language From Within* is supposed to be a Confluent Education "handbook" for teaching English in today's public schools. In reality it has far less to do with English than with philosophy and religion. Says Dr. Galyean, "Confluent Education has as its goal to educate teachers in Gestalt Awareness theory and practice, and to research the results of teachers using these Gestalt strategies in classes."[2] One wonders how many parents would object if they knew that their children were guinea pigs in a government-funded psychotherapeutic experiment to test Gestalt theory! Moreover, Galyean's Eastern religious beliefs are being taught in public schools, where religion is not to be introduced.

If Christianity were being taught in public schools under a similar guise, it would be promptly thrown out. Certainly the ACLU would be up in arms. However, Galyean's and other similar New Age education techniques are accepted in public schools and backed by government funds, even though they condition the students to accept the basic religious beliefs of Hinduism. Very few parents or students recognize what is happening. This conditioning process now going on in public schools across America was described well by C. S. Lewis:

> The process which, if not checked, will abolish Man, goes on apace among Communists and Democrats no less than among Fascists. The methods may (at first) differ in brutality. But many a mild-eyed scientist in pince-nez, many a popular dramatist, many an amateur philosopher in our midst, means in the long run just the same as the Nazi rulers of Germany.
>
> Traditional values are to be "debunked" and mankind to be cut out into some fresh shape at the will (which must, by hypothesis, be an arbitrary will) of some few lucky people in one lucky generation which has learned how to do it.[3]

## Guided Imagery

New Age education leads students into contact with "spirit guides." Dr. Galyean, however, cautions teachers that it is best to call them "imaginary" guides or "wise persons" in public schools. Typical of the method that Galyean and other New Agers teach and which is being widely used in public schools today, beginning in kindergarten, is the following suggestion to be intoned by the teacher:

> Close your eyes and relax. I will lead you in a guided fantasy.
>
> Imagine . . . a very beautiful valley . . . Ahead of you is a mountain . . . you have magic powers so climbing . . . is easy . . . at the top . . . look into the sun and as you do the face of a very wise person slowly appears.
>
> You . . . ask . . . "What must I do to find happiness in my life right now?" The person answers. . . .
>
> When you feel finished with your conversation, come back to us here in the room. Write an account of what was spoken between you and the wise person.[4]

Abuse of the imagination plays a large part because Galyean and other New Age educators are convinced that the students can create their own reality with their minds. Although Galyean sincerely believes that we are each God and therefore have within us all knowledge and wisdom, she adopts the euphemisms "intuition" or "universal consciousness" to hide any religious connotations. Her presentation of Hinduism is usually not recognized as religion, because guided imagery seems so "natural."

## The Transformation of Education

Maria Montessori, founder of the world-famous Montessori schools, was a forerunner of New Age educators. Rejecting the imposition of wisdom from outside, she wanted to free students to be guided by the "inward teacher." She was convinced that this would produce a "New Man . . . able to direct and to mold the future of mankind."[5] Rudolf Steiner, "whose educational philosophy is embodied in the worldwide network of Waldorf schools . . . defined the Waldorf approach as . . . the art of awakening what is actually there within the human being.[6] Well-known educator Jack Canfield states the essence of New Age education in similar terms: "The next step in the transformation of education will be to nurture and value the emergence of what exists innately within the student."[7]

In *The Bridge at Andau*, James Michener relates how escapees from Hungary during the 1956 revolution told him they would stay up all night if necessary to deliver their children from the Communist lies they had been taught that day at school. Parents in America have failed to do the same, unaware of what is happening to their children. While they have slept, Hinduism has been seductively presented to their children as New Age education.

The New Age Movement has a stranglehold on our entire society. Its most strategic work is in the public schools. It is teaching our children that they are gods, and that the only authority they need follow is the "inner light" of their "Higher Self." New Age educators are deliberately trying to bring about a transformation of thinking, morals, world view, and personal identity in public schools across America. It is not honest for them to hide the religious nature of their beliefs. Jack Canfield declares:

> Each person's essential Self knows why it's here and what it needs to learn to further its Soul-purpose. The role of New Age education is to facilitate that inner unfoldment not to impose values and meanings from the outside.[8]

## Truth or Lie?

What Canfield, Galyean, et al are teaching is basic Hinduism. The goal of Hindu Yoga is "Self-realization," to "realize" that one is "God." This is the "truth" that is offered to the one million pitiful creatures who live today in the streets of Calcutta, where they were born and will die, suffering unspeakable poverty, misery, and disease. Hinduism teaches that by the practice of Yoga they can achieve a "higher" state of consciousness, where they will "realize" that the physical universe, including their abject misery, is an illusion (maya) and they are really gods.

This is the "ancient wisdom" we have embraced from the gurus and Yogis who have brought it to America! Hinduism has turned India, in spite of its vast natural resources and manpower, into one of the poorest and most suffering countries on earth. It could do the same to America, if we continue down this path.

New Age leader John White, author of more than 200 articles in such prestigious periodicals as *Reader's Digest* and *Science Digest*, declares: "Our present world situation is a crisis of consciousness . . . the solution [is] . . . very simple: change consciousness."[9] *The Next Whole Earth Catalog* declares: "We are as Gods and might as well get good at it. . . ." In explaining the basis for her philosophy of New Age education, Beverly Galyean states:

> Once we begin to see that we are all God, that we all have the attributes of God, then I think the whole purpose of human life is to reown the Godlikeness within us; the perfect love, the perfect wisdom, the perfect understanding, the perfect intelligence, and when we do that, we create back to that old, that essential oneness which is consciousness. . . .
>
> Confluent education as I work with it is totally dependent on that view, because my whole philosophy is that learning is . . . looking within and discovering what information is inside you . . . [10]

In his famous poem, "The Immortal Friend," world-renowned Hindu philosopher Jiddu Krishnamurti sets out on his "guided imagery" journey to find that same "wise person" that American students are being conditioned to seek. Krishnamurti eventually finds his "friend" in the same place that students in America's public schools are finding theirs—within. The closing lines of the poem express the essence of Hinduism and the New Age:

> My search is at an end.
> In Thee I behold all things.
> I, myself, am God.

That is either the most important truth, the greatest discovery one can make, or else it is the most cruel hoax, the most blatant and destructive lie in the universe! The promise of godhood is first found at the very beginning of the Bible, in Genesis chapter 3. It is the offer that Satan, speaking through a serpent,* makes to Eve. According to the Bible, this was the Lie of lies that destroyed Eve and her descendants, and the human race has never escaped its seductive influence.

---

* For a discussion of the historicity, scientific validity, and meaning of the serpent in Genesis 3 and in modern society, see Dave Hunt, *The Cult Explosion* (Eugene, Oregon: Harvest House Publishers, 1980), pp. 109-15.

# 4

# *Escape from Delusion*

Human history has been an ongoing battle between God and Satan for the souls and destiny of mankind. God's weapon is truth. Satan's weapon is the Lie of no moral absolutes, infinite human potential, and evolution to godhood, which he embellishes with any deception that will best seduce the individual or culture at any given time. The human race has been so thoroughly seduced that this Lie of lies permeates nearly every institution and has become the cornerstone of every human religion. The Judeo-Christian faith alone opposes it. Materialistic science has even succumbed. Atheism or secular humanism, with its declaration that there is no God and that man decides everything for himself, was always just a more devious way of deifying man, while pretending not to be religious.

## Unveiling the Seduction Process

Humans are not just emotional beings but are

also rational beings. Even in our love, joy, pleasure, ecstasy, and mystical experiences, whether on drugs or Yoga, science fiction or worship of idols, we cannot escape the reasoning process. Eastern mysticism is an attempt to do this, but it fails. Even the Yogi backs his experience of so-called pure consciousness with a philosophy. In all of his books recounting his fantastic seductions by Don Juan into the sorcerer's world, Carlos Castaneda continues to reason and build a surrealistic explanation of it all.

We are not robots. If humans have been seduced with Satan's own lie, as the Bible indicates, then we should see the same steps toward the explanation of it being taken again and again in each generation. And we should also discover that we are like Alice in Wonderland, captivated by a delusion that does not really make sense, yet strangely seduced by the garbled rationale supporting it. It can hardly be chance that this is exactly what we discover by looking beneath the popular catch phrases.

If the ultimate truth behind the universe is God Himself, who is infinite and therefore beyond our proud but finite grasp, then every field of knowledge we explore must ultimately resolve itself into a faith system. Science cannot provide, much less prove, ultimate truth. Einstein said that the more science discovers about the universe, the more we are driven to a conclusion concerning its origin that only faith can grasp. Yet faith itself involves a choice between the truth and the Lie. If we choose to put our faith in anything except God, we are doomed. And it is right here, in the very concept and application of faith itself, that we see the human race following the same proud and rebellious steps that Satan himself took. No stronger evidence could be given that this Lie has permeated the very soul of mankind.

The seduction is so powerful that it even takes key statements about faith from the lips of Jesus Himself as its starting point in arriving at the Lie. To a woman whom He healed, Jesus said, "Your faith has made you well."[1] And to His disciples He said, "If you have faith and do not doubt, you shall . . . say to this mountain, 'Be taken up and cast into the sea,' [and] it shall happen."[2] These statements become the basis for focusing upon faith instead of upon the One in whom we are to place our faith. Jesus taught: "Have faith in God."[3] Yet popular faith teacher Kenneth Hagin titled a booklet "Having Faith in Your Faith."[4]

Such teaching implies that prayers are necessarily answered *because we believe*, not because *God* graciously chooses to act on our behalf. If something happens *because we believe it will happen*, then it does not matter *what* or *in whom* we believe—we can make anything happen by *believing*. Since we can decide whether and what to believe, then we can decide our own destiny and create our own universe with our minds. Consequently, we must each be God. One's ultimate goal would then be to get in touch with one's true Self, or the God within. It would follow that God, Buddha, Jesus, Krishna, tarot cards, crystal balls, and the zodiac are all the same thing called by different names: placebos that activate the Force in our minds.

## Problems in Wonderland

It is reasonable and factual to acknowledge that what we believe affects us and our world in many ways. It is unreasonable and fanciful, however, to imagine that our minds create all reality—that if everyone would only think positive thoughts about health and good crops, then all disease and famine would go away. Yogis and various other mystics have been saying for centuries that the universe has no reality but is only an illusion created by our minds. That this mystical view is not true should be evident. Otherwise, how would two scientists, one Chinese and the other American, separated by 10,000 miles and looking through microscopes independently of each other, see the same thing or discover the same virus?

Germs, disease, death, and the intricate universe within a single cell are not inventions of human minds, but exist independently of our thinking. Obviously our thinking determines our perception of the universe; but our perception does not affect the object itself that we are perceiving. This is obvious from the fact that several observers may each simultaneously perceive the same object differently. We ought to be thankful that our minds do not create the world in which we live, in spite of such teaching by mind control cults.

Children dream of a magical Alice-in-Wonderland world where the power of *thinking* creates whatever one wishes. However, such a wonderland would not be a dream, but a nightmare. Just imagine the chaos if there were no laws of physics or chemistry, for example, but everything was in a state of flux and took on shapes and qualities and functions that shifted and blurred in a surrealistic pandemonium of kaleidoscopic pseudo-existence with the changing moods and whims of humans creating it all with their positive or negative thinking!

If we all had Godlike powers, there would simply be too many Gods shuffling "reality" around to suit themselves and in the process conflicting with other Gods, whose minds were imposing a different form upon "reality" according to their taste. Not only is a Creator-God essential for the universe to exist, but any more than one God is too many and would result in chaos. Nevertheless, to exercise these dreamed-of mysterious powers has always been the secret ambition of the human race.

The human claim to godhood has a huge obstacle in God's very obvious physical laws. One would have to be insane to jump out of an airplane under the delusion that a belief in the law of gravity is narrow-minded dogmatism. This is why the use of black or white magic to seemingly violate these laws is practiced in secret, which is the meaning of the word "occult."

In the moral realm, the consequences of breaking God's laws (which eventually break us, since we cannot really break them) are not always obvious or immediate, because this involves the freedom of choice which God has given us. He will not violate that freedom by force. It is in the moral area, then, that the seduction of the Lie bears its most horrible fruit, after we have attempted to play God for a time. Jeremiah said, "The heart is deceitful above all things, and desperately wicked."[5] Jesus declared: "For out of the heart come evil thoughts, murders, adulteries, fornications, thefts, false witness, slanders. These are the things which defile the man."[6]

## The Solution

The gospel declares that the only remedy is to give ourselves to Jesus Christ, believing that He died for our sins and rose again, and to invite Him to come into and cleanse our hearts. We must receive Him as Savior and Lord. "Too simplistic!" complains the psychologist; "Narrow-minded dogmatism!" cries the liberal. Yet both would be stunned if, after being examined by a doctor for a serious problem and asking for the results, the doctor replied: "I'm not so narrow-minded and dogmatic as to come up with a *definite* diagnosis. I would not want to push 'my truth' on you. What would you like? Open-heart surgery has been popular lately, or I could transplant a kidney. I believe that every person is entitled to the operation of his choice." Of course this is absurd.

Yet when it comes to diagnosing society and establishing a basis for eternal destiny through a right relationship with God, suddenly everyone gets "broad-minded" and insists that God should have no principles of His own, but that He should go along with whatever we choose, as long as we are "sincere" about it. Others, unwilling to come to the cross, turn Jesus Christ into a

heavenly Psychiatrist, with whom they can end-
lessly discuss their problems without accepting
what He so plainly said: "If anyone wishes to
come after Me, let him deny himself, and take up
his cross, and follow Me."[7]

Unless there is a correct diagnosis of the evil
plaguing humanity and a genuine cure, there is
no hope. Paul said, "For I am not ashamed of the
gospel [that Christ died for our sins, was buried
and rose the third day from the dead],[8] for it is
the power of God for salvation to everyone who
believes."[9] Christians must stand firmly on this
simple truth and declare it boldly and earnestly
to the world. If out of fear of offending someone
who believes differently we encourage the idea
that a humanistic faith in ourselves and the brave
pulling on bootstraps will eventually produce a
utopian New Age, we are contributing to the
deception of those we mislead.

We must be certain that the Christ we pro-
claim is clearly distinguished from the New Age
false Christs around us. A gospel of self-esteem,
self-worth, and self-acceptance may cause the
unrepentant to feel good about themselves, but
if we do not persuade people that the gospel
must be accepted because it is *true*, and must be
believed and embraced on God's terms, we are
deluding both them and ourselves. We must not
fail to warn those who reject Jesus Christ as Lord
and Savior that they are consigning themselves
to eternal separation from God through the Lie
they have believed—the Lie that dooms forever.

# NOTES

## Chapter One: A New World Order

1. Mark Satin, *New Age Politics: Healing Self and Society* (New York, 1978), pp. 11, 148, 149.
2. Virginia Kay Miller, "Is Nuclear War in Our Future?" in *Whole Life Times*, July/Aug. 1982, pp. 37-38.
3. Lessica Lipnack and Jeffrey Stamps, *Networking: The First Report and Directory*, as quoted in *Whole Life Times*, July/Aug. 1982., p. 49.
4. Ibid.
5. Ibid.
6. Ibid. pp. 213-28.
7. Marilyn Ferguson, *The Aquarian Conspiracy: Personal and Social Transformation in the 1980s* (Los Angeles, 1980), p. 23.
8. International Cooperative Council, *Directory For A New World* (Los Angeles, 1979), p. 299.
9. Ibid.
10. Ferguson, op. cit., pp. 23-25.
11. Paul Robinson, "The Coming of Unenlightenment," in *Psychology Today*, Feb. 1980, pp. 108-14.
12. Fritjof Capra, from a speech at Santa Barbara, CA, the Mind and Supermind Series, Santa Barbara Community College, May 3, 1982.
13. *Los Angeles Times*, Mar. 16, 1982.
14. Ibid.
15. Ibid.
16. *SCP Newsletter*, Aug./Sep. 1982, p. 5.

## Chapter 2: Health, Self, and Science

1. *Los Angeles Times*, July 12, 1981.
2. Ibid.
3. Ibid.
4. Ibid.
5. *Brain/Mind Bulletin*, Oct. 4, 1982, p.2.
6. Ferguson, op. cit., pp. 241-42.
7. Ibid., pp. 99-101.
8. Martin L. Gross, *The Pschological Society* (New York, 1978), pp. 4-5.
9. Carl G. Jung, *Two Essays on Analytical Psychology*.
10. Abraham Maslow, *Main Currents in Modern Thought*.

11. Ferguson, op. cit., pp. 340-342.
12. *Self Acceptance: Real Encounter,* front page; *Questions and Answers About Lifespring,* p. 3; *The Family News,* Vol. 1, No. 2, July 1978, p. 14.
13. Elmer and Alyce Green, *Beyond Biofeedback* (New York, 1979), pp. 56, 342-43.
14. *Los Angeles Times,* Sep. 4, 1981, Business p. 1.
15. Ibid.
16. Ibid.
17. *SCP Journal,* July 1977.
18. Simon & Schuster promotional material for *The Turning Point.*

## Chapter 3: New Age Education
1. C. S. Lewis, *The Abolition of Man* (New York, 1947), pp. 16-17.
2. Beverly Galyean, *Language From Within* (Long Beach, CA, 1976), p.1
3. C. S. Lewis, op. cit. p. 85.
4. Galyean, op. cit., p. 91.
5. Dori Smith, "Education for the Future: Eliciting the Spark from Within," in *Whole Life Times,* Sep./Oct. 1982.
6. Ibid.
7. *Whole Life Times,* Apr./May 1982, Los Angeles Directory, p. 1.
8. Ibid.
9. International Cooperative Council, *Directory For A New World* (Los Angeles, 1979), p. 12.
10. *SCP Journal,* Winter 1981-82, pp. 29, 31.

## Chapter 4: Escape from Delusion
1. Matthew 9:22.
2. Matthew 21:21.
3. Mark 11:22.
4. Kenneth E. Hagin, "Having Faith in Your Faith," in *The Word of Faith,* Sep. 1980, p. 3.
5. Jeremiah 17:9 KJV.
6. Matthew 15:19,20.
7. Mark 8:34.
8. 1 Corinthians 15:1-8.
9. Romans 1:16.

# *Harvest Pocket Books*

These compact pocket books are excerpted from best-selling, full-length Harvest House books. Each booklet gives the major thrust of the complete book in an inexpensive, condensed version, designed for readers on the go. Further material on each topic can be obtained by purchasing the full-length edition.

Dear Reader:

We would appreciate hearing from you regarding this Harvest House pocket book. It will enable us to continue to give you the best in Christian publishing.

1. What most influenced you to purchase *Understanding the New Age Movement*?
   - ☐ Author
   - ☐ Subject matter
   - ☐ Backcover copy
   - ☐ Recommended
   - ☐ Cover/Title
   - ☐ _____

2. Your overall rating of this book:
   ☐ Excellent ☐ Very good ☐ Good ☐ Fair ☐ Poor

3. How likely would you be to purchase other books by this author?
   - ☐ Very likely
   - ☐ Somewhat likely
   - ☐ Not very likely
   - ☐ Not at all

4. After reading this Harvest House Pocket Book would you be inclined to purchase the complete book, *Peace, Prosperity, and the Coming Holocaust*?
   ☐ Yes ☐ No

5. What types of books most interest you? (check all that apply)
   - ☐ Women's Books
   - ☐ Marriage Books
   - ☐ Current Issues
   - ☐ Self Help/Psychology
   - ☐ Bible Studies
   - ☐ Fiction
   - ☐ Biographies
   - ☐ Children's Books
   - ☐ Youth Books
   - ☐ Other _____

6. Please check the box next to your age group.
   - ☐ Under 18
   - ☐ 18-24
   - ☐ 25-34
   - ☐ 35-44
   - ☐ 45-54
   - ☐ 55 and over

**Mail to:** Editorial Director
Harvest House Publishers
1075 Arrowsmith
Eugene, OR 97402

Name _____

Address _____

City _____ State _____ Zip _____

**Thank you for helping us to help you
in future publications!**